# FLOOD

*Two modern boats continue the old tradition of steamboat races on the Mississippi.*

# FLOOD
## WRESTLING WITH THE MISSISSIPPI

By Patricia Lauber

**NATIONAL
GEOGRAPHIC
SOCIETY**
Washington, D.C.

Distributed by Publishers Group West

Copyright © 1996 by Patricia Lauber

## PUBLISHED BY THE NATIONAL GEOGRAPHIC SOCIETY

Reg Murphy, President and Chief Executive Officer

Gilbert M. Grosvenor, Chairman of the Board

Nina D. Hoffman, Senior Vice President

William R. Gray, Vice President and Director of the Book Division

Barbara Lalicki, Director of Children's Publishing

Barbara Brownell, Senior Editor—Mark A. Caraluzzi, Marketing Manager

Staff for this book:

Suez Kehl, Art Director—Greta Arnold, Illustrations Editor—Carl Mehler, Map Editor

Vincent P. Ryan, Manufacturing Manager—Lewis R. Bassford, Production Manager

Corinne Szabo, Picture Researcher—Tracey M. Wood, Map Researcher—James Huckenpahler, Map Production

Anne Marie Houppert, Indexer—Meredith Wilcox, Illustrations Assistant—Dale Herring—Editorial Assistant

1145 17TH ST. N.W.
WASHINGTON, D.C. 20036

Library of Congress Cataloguing in Publication Data

Lauber, Patricia
    Flood : wrestling with the Mississippi / by Patricia Lauber.
        p.        cm.
    Includes index.
    Summary: Describes the history of flooding of the Mississippi River, focusing on the
1927 and 1993 floods, the effects on people near the river, and efforts to avoid flooding.
    ISBN 0-7922-4141-X
    1. Floods--Mississippi River--Juvenile literature. (1. Floods--Mississippi River.) 1. Title
    GB1399.4.M72L38 1996
    363.3'493'0977--dc20                                              95-47338
                                                                      CIP

DISTRIBUTED BY PUBLISHERS GROUP WEST
P.O. Box 8843
Emeryville, California 94662

# Contents

*Early in its journey to the Gulf of Mexico, the Mississippi River meanders—twists and turns—through the marshes of northern Minnesota.*

# 1
# Big River

For THOUSANDS OF YEARS THE BIG RIVER ran free. Flowing south, it gathered the waters of many other rivers. With those waters came sand and soil scoured from channels and banks. Where the big river moved fast, it carried along the sand and soil—the sediment. Where the river slowed, sediment settled out of it.

One place where the river slowed was at its mouth. Here, where it met the sea, it dropped millions of tons of sediment every year. In time, the sediment rose above the sea, forming land that is called a delta.

Sometimes an early spring caused a sudden melting of winter snows. Sometimes heavy rains fell. Then there were floods. The river swelled, jumped its banks, and spread out over the land. Slowing, the waters dropped sediment. The sediment built a plain, a floodplain of rich soil.

The river traveled its floodplain in sweeping curves and horseshoe bends. It often changed its course, cutting off old bends and forming new ones.

It built sandbars, then shifted them around. From time to time it found a new and shorter route to the sea and built another delta.

This river was the Mississippi: big, powerful, a builder of land.

THE DRAINAGE BASIN OF THE MISSISSIPPI REACHES INTO 31 STATES AND 2 CANADIAN PROVINCES.

THE MISSISSIPPI rises as a small stream in Minnesota. Flowing out of Lake Itasca, it travels 2,340 miles to the Gulf of Mexico. From its source, the Mississippi ambles along for miles, flowing northeast through a wilderness. It turns east, then finally south, rambling through forests and speeding over waterfalls. Small streams and rivers flow into it.

By the time it reaches Minneapolis and St. Paul, Minnesota, the Mississippi has

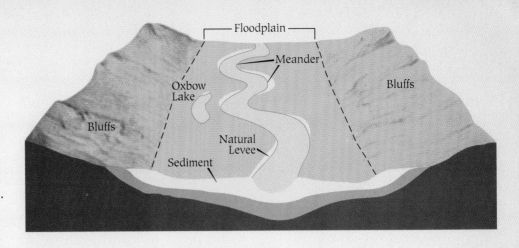

Floodplain

Meander

Oxbow
Lake

Bluffs

Bluffs

Natural
Levee

Sediment

A FLOODPLAIN IS THE FLAT
LAND BESIDE A RIVER THAT
FLOODS WHEN THE RIVER
OVERFLOWS ITS BANKS.
AS WATER SPREADS OUT, IT
SLOWS, DROPPING THE
SEDIMENT IT WAS CARRYING.

grown greatly. It speeds up, growing still more as it takes in the waters of large rivers. In this part of its course, the Mississippi flows through a narrow valley. The floodplain is five to ten miles wide and edged by lofty bluffs.

At Cape Girardeau, some 1,300 miles from its source, the Mississippi enters a vast valley that slopes gently toward the Gulf. Built of sediment, the valley is some 600 miles long and 60 to 130 miles wide. The Mississippi made this land by filling in what was once an arm of the sea.

*Clarks Fork, tumbling down the Rockies, feeds the Yellowstone River, which feeds the Missouri, which feeds the Mississippi.*

The rivers that join the Mississippi along its route are called its tributaries. The two biggest are the Missouri and the Ohio. The Missouri, longest river in North America, is a tide of swirling brown water that joins the Mississippi above Cape Girardeau. The Ohio joins the Mississippi below the Cape, at Cairo, Illinois. It adds the largest burden of water, more than doubling the amount in the Mississippi. The big river becomes a giant.

The tributaries have their own tributaries, which also have tributaries. Sooner or later, the waters of perhaps 100,000 rivers and streams drain into the Mississippi. On a map they look like an enormous spider web reaching into 31 states and 2 Canadian provinces.

9

*La Salle, an early French explorer of North America, greets Taensa Indians in what is now Louisiana. He claimed the basin of the Mississippi for France in 1682.*

The first people to know the river were Native Americans. They named it *Mississippi*, meaning "Big River" or "Father of Waters." They gathered plants from its floodplain, hunted beside it, fished its waters, and traveled it in canoes. They had seen the river in flood and, when possible, made their homes on high ground. Sometimes they moved away until the floodwaters went down.

The first Europeans to settle beside the Mississippi were French. In 1718 they began building the city we call New Orleans. In many ways the site seemed ideal. It was surrounded by rich farmland. Furs and timber from the northern wilderness could be rafted down the Mississippi to New Orleans, then loaded on ocean-going ships. There was only one problem. The site was likely to be flooded.

And so the French built a wall of earth, a levee, between themselves and the river. When finished, the levee was more than a mile long, 4 feet high, and 18 feet wide at the top. That levee was the first human attempt to wrestle with the Mississippi and to tame it. It was also the first of many levees to be built.

In the years that followed, great changes took place along the river. With

THE LOUISIANA PURCHASE DOUBLED THE SIZE OF THE YOUNG UNITED STATES, WHICH WAS LARGELY EAST OF THE MISSISSIPPI RIVER. MAP SHOWS TODAY'S STATE BORDERS.

*Snag boats removed tree trunks and other large objects from the river to keep it open for shipping.*

the Louisiana Purchase in 1803, land claimed by France became part of the young United States. Cotton plantations covered the delta. The invention of the steamboat meant that goods and people could easily travel up the river as well as down. The floodplain, with some of the richest soil in the world, became farmland. Farms were served by towns that sprang up along the river and thrived on its traffic. Industries were drawn to the river for its fresh water and shipping. The U. S. Army Corps of Engineers kept the river open, dredging canals and removing snags.

As people moved west and clustered along the river, they built levees. Even so, the Mississippi flooded time and again, breaking through levees, swamping towns, spreading over its floodplain. Each time the levees were repaired. Each time even more levees were built. During the mid- and late 1800s, some 1,500 miles of levees were built along the lower Mississippi by men with shovels and wheelbarrows. In the upper valley, farmers and other settlers built their own levees to hold the river in its channel.

With the invention of the steamboat, the Mississippi became a water highway that reached between Minneapolis and St. Paul (above) in Minnesota to New Orleans (below). New Orleans, at the river's mouth, became a busy international port.

*Floods were a common problem in early days along the Mississippi.*
*Here, with its gangplank lowered, a big paddle wheeler waits to rescue a settler who is*
*loading his belongings into two skiffs. A pair of mules and a cow are on the porch,*
*trying to escape this flood of the early 1880s.*

By the 1900s, levees were bigger and stronger than ever before. And still the floods continued. The Mississippi often seemed like a living thing, with a mind of its own, going where it wanted to go and doing what it wanted to do. Where it wanted to go at high water was onto its ancient floodplain.

And that is where it went in the summer of 1993. That year brought the worst flood ever to strike the upper valley. Swollen by seemingly endless rains, the Mississippi exploded through levees, spilled over the land, and snatched back huge pieces of its floodplain in the Middle West.

*Rain fell, seemingly without end, in the summer of 1993. Residents of Cedar Rapids struggled in a flash flood caused by the swollen Cedar River, which feeds the Iowa River, which feeds the Mississippi.*

# 2
# Endless Rain

SPRING OF 1992 BROUGHT DROUGHT. Across Iowa and other states of the upper Middle West, farmland dried into a crumbly crust. In early July, the skies finally darkened and rain began to fall. People rejoiced.

But once started, the rains didn't stop. All summer long, it rained and rained and rained. Summer was also cooler than usual. High above the earth there was haze in the atmosphere, caused by a volcanic eruption in the Philippines. The haze cut off some of the sun's rays. Less water was drawn back into the atmosphere. More stayed on the land, soaking it through and through.

Autumn was rainy.

Winter of 1992-93 brought heavy rains.

Spring brought storms.

As the rain-filled spring crept by, people began to worry. Rivers were rising steadily between their levees. The mighty Mississippi was swollen and rushing. So were its tributaries, the many rivers and streams that added their waters to the big river.

In June worry changed to alarm. The ground had long since soaked up all the water it could hold. The only place

*A levee on the Illinois River near St. Louis forms an arch in this photograph. The barrier stretching across the arch was placed there in case the levee was overtopped during the 1993 flood.*

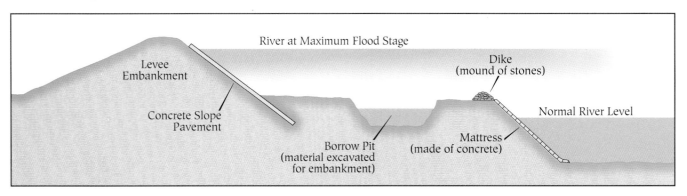

River at Maximum Flood Stage

Levee Embankment

Dike (mound of stones)

Concrete Slope Pavement

Normal River Level

Borrow Pit (material excavated for embankment)

Mattress (made of concrete)

A TYPICAL MISSISSIPPI RIVER VALLEY LEVEE SYSTEM

rainwater could go was into the rapidly rising creeks, streams, and rivers.

There had been floods before, times when main streets filled with water and farmland turned into lakes. Each time people cleaned up, rebuilt, and went on with their lives. Some flooding, they felt, was a price they had to pay for farming the rich soil of a floodplain.

Over the years defenses had been strengthened. Cities had concrete floodwalls and levees armored with concrete, built by the Corps of Engineers. Earthen levees built by local groups were higher and longer. To hold back water, the Corps had built dams and reservoirs on some tributaries of the Mississippi. All this work had one aim: to keep the river in its channel so that people could safely live and work on the floodplain.

Would the defenses hold? In early summer of 1993, people could only wonder—and worry. No one could remember seeing the river rise so high. Nor had anyone ever seen such rain. Even if a day started fair, by afternoon storm clouds were building up again. Nights were shattered by bolts of lightning, claps of thunder, and the drumming of rain on roofs.

Weather scientists could explain what was happening, but they could not offer much hope. Winds high in the atmosphere were steering hot, moist air into the upper Midwest. There the air collided with cold air from Canada. The cold caused moisture to condense out of the warm air and fall as rain. Usually, storms broke up and moved east. In 1993 they could not. They were blocked by a mass of hot, dry air over the East Coast. Until that mass of air

*St. Louis, with its Gateway Arch, was one of the cities with a floodwall. The 11-mile-long concrete wall was built by the Corps of Engineers.*

**By early July, a sea of water surrounded this farm
in north St. Charles County, Missouri.**

moved out to sea, rain would go on falling and falling on the Midwest. Sometimes 5 to 12 inches fell in a single day.

By the middle of July, rain had fallen on the Midwest for 49 straight days. And by then rivers had been bursting through levees, spreading over farms and towns. A satellite picture showed much of Iowa colored blue, as if it were one of the Great Lakes. In eight states, rivers had taken back 15 million acres of farmland and driven 36,000 people from their homes.

Along the Mississippi the worst flooding took place between Davenport, Iowa, and the area south of St. Louis, Missouri. Here there were no reservoirs or lakes to hold back water. And here the Mississippi received the waters of several large tributaries—the Iowa, the Des Moines, the Illinois, and the Missouri. On July 19, there were floods along 464 miles of the Mississippi, from McGregor, Iowa, to St. Louis.

SATELLITE IMAGES SHOW THE DIFFERENCE BETWEEN NORMAL SUMMER WATER LEVELS OF THE MISSISSIPPI AND MISSOURI RIVERS (LEFT) AND THOSE OF THE 1993 FLOOD (RIGHT). THE MISSISSIPPI AND ILLINOIS RIVERS ARE AT THE TOP OF THE IMAGES, THE MISSOURI AT THE LEFT.

*At Sny Island, sandbagging went on day and night. Workers formed human chains...as they did (center) at Prairie du Rocher,*

## THE SNY ISLAND LEVEE

As the Mississippi twists and turns out of Iowa and into Missouri and Illinois, it is fairly narrow—only 1,500 feet wide at some points. Nearing Quincy, Illinois, it can carry 250,000 cubic feet of water a second without flooding. In the summer of 1993, it was carrying more than twice that amount.

The town of Quincy stands on bluffs, high above the Mississippi. It looks out over 110,000 acres of fertile farmlands, up and down the river. All are part of a levee district named Sny Island.

In late spring of 1993, farm buildings and fields of corn and soybeans lay snug behind a 54-mile-long levee. But the men and women who worked and lived there were watching the river. Since April it had been high, as it often was after winter snow had melted. But the water had always gone down

*Pigs, rescued from the roof of a barn, are lifted into a boat at Kaskaskia, Illinois. On the Mississippi itself, the worst flooding took place between Davenport, Iowa, and the area south of St. Louis.*

*Illinois. Volunteers from all over the country helped.*

as summer arrived. This year it didn't. Instead, it began to rise, slowly but steadily. In late June one of Quincy's two bridges to Missouri was closed. The Missouri end, which had no levees, was underwater.

A thunderstorm raged during the night of Wednesday, June 30. It dumped six inches of rain on Quincy and more to the north. The river rose two feet. People began to wonder whether the levee would hold. In 120 years, it had had only one serious break. But it had never faced a test like this one.

By Thursday morning small creeks had flooded roads, and the river was rising steadily. The Sny levee stood 28 feet above the river channel. The normal height of the river was 11 feet. On the morning of July 1, it was about a foot below the top of the levee and rising an inch an hour. Water was seeping through the base of the levee. And the National Weather Service was predicting that a crest of water 30 feet high would pass Quincy on Saturday, July 3.

People of the floodplain loaded cars and trucks with their belongings—sofas, TV sets, refrigerators, rugs, desks—to be stored with friends or relatives on higher ground. Farm animals were trucked away to be boarded or sent to market.

A call went out for helpers, trucks, bulldozers, and sandbags. The levee had to be raised and strengthened.

One section was a weak link. During the 1960s most of the Sny was rebuilt, using large amounts of sand. When a levee needs to be raised, wet sand can be bulldozed from its base up the side and will stay in place. Wet earth does not. Bulldozed toward the top, it slides back to the base. For some reason, one mile-long section had not been rebuilt. It was still made of earth. There was only one way to raise it: build a wall of wooden boards along its top and support the wall with beams and sandbags.

Farmers began arriving, some from high ground miles away. Most were strangers, but help was needed and so they came, driving bulldozers and trucks. Over the next three weeks, hundreds of other strangers would also volunteer to help raise the Sny levee and work on the weak link.

All day long that first day, men and women hauled wood, sawed it, and hammered it. They worked in 95° heat, high humidity, swarms of mosquitoes, and never-ending mud. By evening stretches of board were rising on top of the weak link. Work went on into the night, and by 3 a.m. the first section of boards and beams was in place. Now it had to be backed by thousands of sandbags. Each one needed to be filled, moved along the levee, and put in place by hand.

The river was only inches below the top of the old levee. With no time to waste, everyone was up early and back at work.

Work continued into the night. Somewhere upstream a levee gave way and water poured off the river onto the floodplain. At Sny Island the

*When this levee gave way, Valmeyer, Illinois, was swamped.*

*At the Sny, as at other levees, sandbags had to be filled before they could be used.*    *At East Dubuque, Illinois, it was too*

pressure eased, and the river seemed to be holding steady at just under 28 feet. When work stopped, 42,000 sandbags, each weighing 30 to 40 pounds, had been put in place.

Sunday, July 4, brought heavy rain to the Midwest. The Weather Service forecast that a crest of 31.5 feet would pass Quincy on July 11. That meant the mile-long board fence had to be raised. The governor of Illinois called in the National Guard to help.

Late on the afternoon of July 9, another levee gave way upstream and water rushed over 10,000 acres. At Sny Island the river began to drop, but heavy rains were still falling over Iowa and other parts of the Midwest, draining off the land, swelling rivers, and rushing toward the Mississippi. The Weather Service now forecast a crest of 32.5 feet at Quincy on Wednesday, July 14. The board fence had to be raised again.

By Tuesday morning the fence had been raised. Workers in human chains were passing and placing sandbags—adding to the half million already in place. They felt sure of finishing before the crest arrived. Then the sky turned black, the wind rose, and bolts of lightning streaked the sky. For safety's sake, all workers were pulled off the levee. The river was five inches below the top of the boards.

The battle seemed to be lost, but that night two more levees gave way upstream. The river dropped 2 feet. The Weather Service now forecast that the 32.5-foot crest would pass Quincy on Thursday.

*late to hold back the Mississippi.*   *Kaskaskia is an island that for a time appeared as part of the Mississippi.*

On Thursday night the crest came, 32 feet high.  The Sny levee held. The river stayed as high on Friday. The Sny held. Work on the levee now slowed. Workers patrolled, watching for signs of weakness or small leaks. Bulldozers pushed up sand. The river was still pressing against the levee, which was now soggy and weakening.

A week later the river was still at 30 feet. Day and night, farmers watched the Sny. Farmhouses and barns were empty. Corn and soybeans still stretched as far as the eye could see, but it was too early to tell if there would ever be a harvest.

That weekend the rains began again. Slowly the river began to rise. It was one time too many. Part of the Sny levee gave way, not the weak link with the board fence but another part. By evening on Sunday, July 25, 44,000 acres of corn and soybeans lay under 15 feet of water. Only the roofs of houses and barns showed that Sny Island was not a lake. People had done all they could, but it was not enough.

## Up and Down the Valley

In the upper valley of the Mississippi and along its tributaries, town after town suffered in the summer of 1993. The small river town of Alexandria, Missouri, saw the river rise in spring—and go on rising. On July 8, the levee broke and the town went under for the rest of the summer.

Niota, Illinois, was one of several towns helped by prisoners—young, fit, first offenders sentenced for non-violent crimes. They were city men, most of whom had never seen the Mississippi or a farm. At first Niota seemed strange to them. But working shoulder-to-shoulder with local people, they soon came to feel that Niota was their town, too, and they worked with a will. For nine straight days, they threw sandbags from 8 a.m. until dark, in rain, sun, heat, humidity, and mud. The townspeople were awed by how hard they worked. The young prisoners were awed by how nice the townspeople were, thanking them, supplying cold drinks, and feeding them roast beef, chicken, catfish, meatloaf, apple pie, peach cobbler.

At 6 p.m. on July 10, the levee broke. Some of the prisoners cried, as did men and women of Niota. They had done their best, yet the river had won. That last night, the prisoners refused to eat because they had not saved the town.

Davenport, Iowa, had no levees. The city had missed its chance to have the federal government build levees and floodwalls. Later, its citizens decided they could not afford to pay for the work themselves. Besides, they did not want to wall off the river and lose their view. The city suffered widespread flooding.

There were also places where defenses did hold. One was Hannibal, Missouri, boyhood home of Mark Twain. The town had built a levee that stood 31 feet higher than the river bottom. As the water rose, townspeople raised the levee 3 feet with sandbags. The river crested at 32 feet, and Hannibal was safe.

The Missouri joins the Mississippi about 20 miles north of St. Louis. St. Louis was the largest city in harm's way. It was also the first to face the

*During the summer of 1993, farmers of the floodplain watched anxiously as the Mississippi rose ever higher behind its levees.*

26

floodwaters of both the Missouri and the Mississippi. At one time more than 480 million gallons of water a minute churned past the city. But most of the city stayed dry behind its 11-mile-long concrete floodwall. Damage came chiefly from a small tributary that backed up when forced to take water from the Mississippi.

Downriver from St. Louis was Ste. Genevieve, Missouri, which called itself the first settlement west of the Mississippi. It had stood there for 250 years, but in late July its future did not look bright. Its levee rose 36 to 38

*Cairo lies on a point of land where the big Ohio River (right) flows in from the east to join the Mississippi.*

feet above the river bottom; the river was expected to crest at 45 feet. If Ste. Genevieve flooded, it would lose what it most prized: houses made of logs stuck together with clay, animal hair, and straw—the country's best examples of what the French settlers built.

The town's problems began to attract attention on television and in newspapers. From miles away—Colorado, Minnesota, Tennessee, Florida—people decided to help. They piled into buses, cars, and trucks and drove to the small town. All told, some 1,200 volunteers arrived to help. They filled and set in place 1,100,000 sandbags, raising the levee by ten feet. To strengthen it they dumped 100,000 tons of rock behind the sandbags. The old buildings were saved.

Once the floodwaters reached Cape Girardeau and Cairo, they were no longer a problem. The giant lower Mississippi easily swallowed the vast tide that was sweeping south. Its own tributaries were low in the summer of 1993.

# As the Waters Fell

There was no one day when the flood of 1993 ended, no one day when people knew they were safe from the river. But in August the weather pattern began slowly to change. People sensed that the worst was over. Those who had been flooded out yearned to go home. Most were living nearby, crammed in with friends or relatives or in mobile homes that the federal government had brought in. But no one could go home until the water drained back into the river. Rain still fell. Some towns went under a second, or even a third, time. In places, farms still lay under muddy water 11 miles wide and 20 feet deep.

Days were spent making the rounds from one government agency to another, applying for loans, grants, and other kinds of help. In early evening, families might drive to the edge of the water, park, and talk to neighbors. Ahead was the road that used to lead to home; now it dipped under the water and disappeared. Sometimes people would boat into their towns and

*As the waters began to drop, families could visit their towns and farms by boat.*
*This family is looking at the building where it used to store grain.*

float down Main Street. At first there was little to see except a chimney, a TV antenna, the top of a telephone pole. As the water dropped, they began to see the remains of houses—windows blown out, porches sagging.

Finally the time came when they could get into their houses. What many found were mud-caked ruins: eight inches of thick dark mud on the floors, mud on the walls, mud on the ceiling, mud on the furniture. They found mildew, mold, and dead fish. But these were people who had sandbagged for days on end, women who had cooked for hundreds of volunteers and washed their muddy clothes. They were workers. They were people raised to believe that life is good but hard, people raised to believe that you work for what you get. And so they set to work hauling out soggy rugs and couches, ruined refrigerators and TVs, and piling them on lawns covered with slime. With shovels, brooms, and buckets of water and bleach, they

*A father and daughter from Taos, Missouri, used a boat to reach their trailer and swam in through the door to save what little they could.*

*Volunteers also helped with the*

attacked the houses that could be repaired. They might still be cleaning up when the first frost came, but they never doubted. They would be back.

Many of these families had lived on their land or in their small towns for generations. Their roots ran deep. Most hoped to be buried in the place where they had been born, raised, and married. They loved their small towns where they knew everybody, neighbor helped neighbor, and no one ever locked a door. They wanted to keep what they had.

Yet the flood of 1993 raised questions about putting everything back the way it was. Perhaps, some people said, it was time to think again about the ways we wrestle with the Mississippi. Perhaps, they said, we should take a new look at the whole river, for the lower Mississippi Valley has a long history of problems. They are caused by the nature of the Mississippi, by the kind of river it is, and also by the nature of people.

*clean-up. This one is shoveling out a house in Hull, Illinois.*

*A family photo and a banjo clock were among the few items saved from a flooded house.*

*Ready to be rescued from the White River, a group waits patiently on the roof of a house in Wabash, Arkansas, during the 1927 flood.*

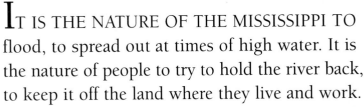

# 3

# Big Changes on a Big River

It IS THE NATURE OF THE MISSISSIPPI TO flood, to spread out at times of high water. It is the nature of people to try to hold the river back, to keep it off the land where they live and work.

For some 200 years along the lower Mississippi, people tried to defend their land with levees. Sometimes the levees worked. Sometimes the river ate through them and took back its floodplain. After each flood, levees were rebuilt, bigger and stronger. And still the river went on flooding. In 1927 it finally became clear that levees alone were not enough. Levees alone could not tame the river, could not pin it in place. That year brought a flood that swamped the lower Mississippi Valley.

The flood was caused by heavy rains that drenched much of the Mississippi's drainage basin from August 1926 through most of the following winter. Rivers rose higher and higher. By early January the Cumberland River, which flows into the Ohio, was 41 feet higher than it had been in August. The Ohio itself was 27 feet higher at Cairo, Illinois, where it joins the Mississippi.

In February the heavy rains seemed to be ending, but in March they began again. A great tide of water crept into the valley of the lower Mississippi. Its crest, a mountain of water, rolled south at 44 miles a day. Levees weakened and burst.

That spring a sea of muddy brown water spread over more than 18.3 million acres in seven states. In places it was 18 feet deep and 80 miles across. Hundreds of people and thousands of animals died. Some 650,000 people were driven from their homes, with thousands marooned on the tops of levees that still stood.

What had gone wrong? The answer had to do with levees, which were then the only defense against flooding. In some ways the levees were making matters worse.

When the river ran free, high waters spread slowly over its floodplain. Now, penned in its channel, the river had no place to go except up. It rose higher and higher, spilling over levees and eating them away. When it found weak spots, it exploded through, bulldozing everything in its path. In 1927, levees broke in more than 120 places between Cairo and the Gulf of Mexico.

When the level of the river finally fell, water was slow to drain off the land. Levees were blocking it.

After the 1927 flood, Congress voted a large sum of money for work along the Mississippi. The Corps of Engineers was put in charge of the work. Levees would be repaired and raised. But it was clearly time for some new ways of dealing with floods of

*Flooding had ended, but the levee at Arkansas City, Arkansas, trapped water in the town. Red Cross boats delivered supplies to people living in tents along the top of the levee.*

water. The engineer in charge summed them up by saying, "The water wants out. We will give it out." The Corps began a vast program of changes to protect the valley.

One way to get water out of the river was to speed up its journey to the Gulf. Along its natural route, the Mississippi often threw out big loops, curving around and almost closing the loop. Later, it might break through and cut off the loop, shortening its own course. The Corps saw places where it could make cutoffs itself. By 1937, it had dug out 64 million cubic yards of earth and shortened the river by some 150 miles. Shorter and straighter, the river cleared itself faster of rising waters and there was less flooding.

To keep the river from making new loops, some of its banks were armored with huge mattresses made of concrete plates.

W HERE NEEDED, riverbanks were armored with what is called a mattress. Earlier mattresses were made of woven willow branches covered with rocks. Modern ones are made of slabs of reinforced concrete, each 4 feet long, 14 inches wide, and 3 inches thick. First the riverbank is scraped smooth and given the right slope. Then workers on a barge join the slabs in 140-by-25-foot units. One end of the unit is anchored to the riverbank at the waterline. The barge backs away, paying out mattress, so that a section of bank is covered to the deepest part of the river's bed. A second mattress is laid next to the first, then a third, and so on. Finally, the upper part of the bank is paved with stone to protect it during floods.

SATELLITE IMAGE SHOWS THE LOWER MISSISSIPPI VALLEY. IN THIS IMAGE, TO WHICH COLOR HAS BEEN ADDED, THE FLOODPLAIN APPEARS PINKISH. THE BLACK LOOPS AND CRESCENTS ARE LAKES LEFT BEHIND WHEN THE RIVER'S COURSE CHANGED. THEY ARE CALLED OXBOWS.

In places, new levees were built five miles back from the riverbanks, allowing high waters to spread out.

New standards were set for the building of levees. Old levees that did not meet the standards were torn down and rebuilt—600 miles of them by 1937.

The Corps also decided to let less water into the upper valley at times of high water. To do this, it built dams and reservoirs on tributaries. Here water could be stored, then released slowly when river levels dropped.

The biggest change of all was to build levees that could be opened during floods. As water escaped, the level of the river would fall. The Engineers started work at Cairo.

Cairo stood on a low neck of land where the Ohio River boiled into the Mississippi. The city was guarded by a floodwall built to hold back water that rose to a height of 60 feet, but it was still a danger spot. The Corps planned to let water out of the Mississippi at Cairo, lead it away, and then put it back in the river 30 miles downstream.

The levee on the west side of the river was rebuilt. The new levee had two fuse plugs—sections that were lower than the rest of the levee. If the river threatened to rise to more than 55 feet, the fuse plugs could be made lower by removing their upper layers, to let water flow away from Cairo.

Ten miles to the west, another levee was built. The area between the two levees was a floodway, a place for floodwaters to go. The floodway led the water south to New Madrid, Missouri, and put it back into the Mississippi.

New Orleans was another danger spot. The city was low-lying and nearly surrounded by water—the Mississippi River and Lake Pontchartrain. To guard New Orleans the Corps built a floodway to take water out of the river, lead it to Lake Pontchartrain, and send it into the Gulf of Mexico.

Upstream from New Orleans, the Engineers built a 7,000-foot-long, concrete spillway with 350 wooden bays. If all were opened, two million gallons of water a second could pass into the floodway and Lake Pontchartrain.

Early in 1937 the new plan faced its first test.

January brought 25 days of rain that fell in torrents. Fifteen trillion gallons of water drenched the drainage basin of the Ohio River. Along its

*Bays in the Bonnet Carre Spillway at Lake Ponchartrain can be opened or closed by cranes that remove or replace huge timbers called needles.*

length, the Ohio rose and jumped its banks. It dumped a sea of water into the Mississippi. At Cairo, the Mississippi was rising rapidly, overtopping the levee. A crest of 63 feet was predicted.

There was no time to waste. On January 25, the Corps blasted an opening in the fuse-plug levee. One fourth of the Mississippi's waters ran off into the new floodway. By afternoon river levels at Cairo were dropping. The city was safe.

Downstream, the levees were holding. But it was clear that the swollen river would top the levees at New Orleans. One by one, 285 bays in the spillway were opened. Floodwaters poured into Lake Pontchartrain, enough to cover 1.25 million acres to a depth of 10 feet. New Orleans stayed dry.

People did die in the 1937 flood. Thousands of homes were destroyed and millions of acres of farmland flooded. But this time most of the damage was not along the Mississippi, where the main levees held. It was done by the Ohio or by the Mississippi's waters backing into other tributaries.

Even so, the big river was far from tamed. The Mississippi was threatening to change its route to the Gulf, to swing west, away from Baton Rouge and New Orleans. If it did, most of its water would reach the Gulf through a river called the Atchafalaya (ah-chaf-uh-LIE-yuh).

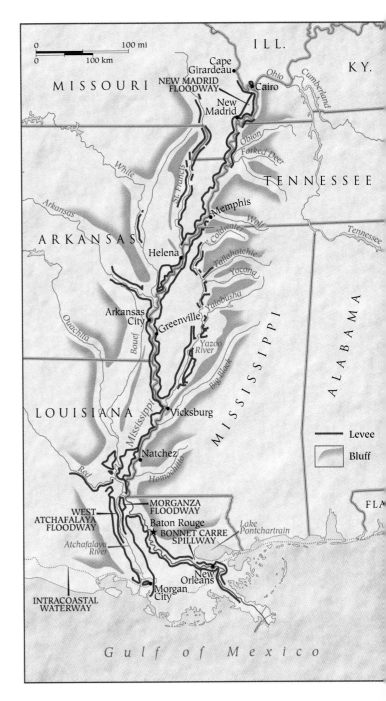

THE LOWER MISSISSIPPI AND PARTS OF ITS TRIBUTARIES ARE HELD ON COURSE BY LEVEES. WHEN FLOODS THREATEN CAIRO, WATER CAN BE RELEASED FROM THE MISSISSIPPI TO FLOW DOWN A FLOODWAY. IT IS PUT BACK INTO THE RIVER AT NEW MADRID. THE BONNET CARRE SPILLWAY PROTECTS NEW ORLEANS.

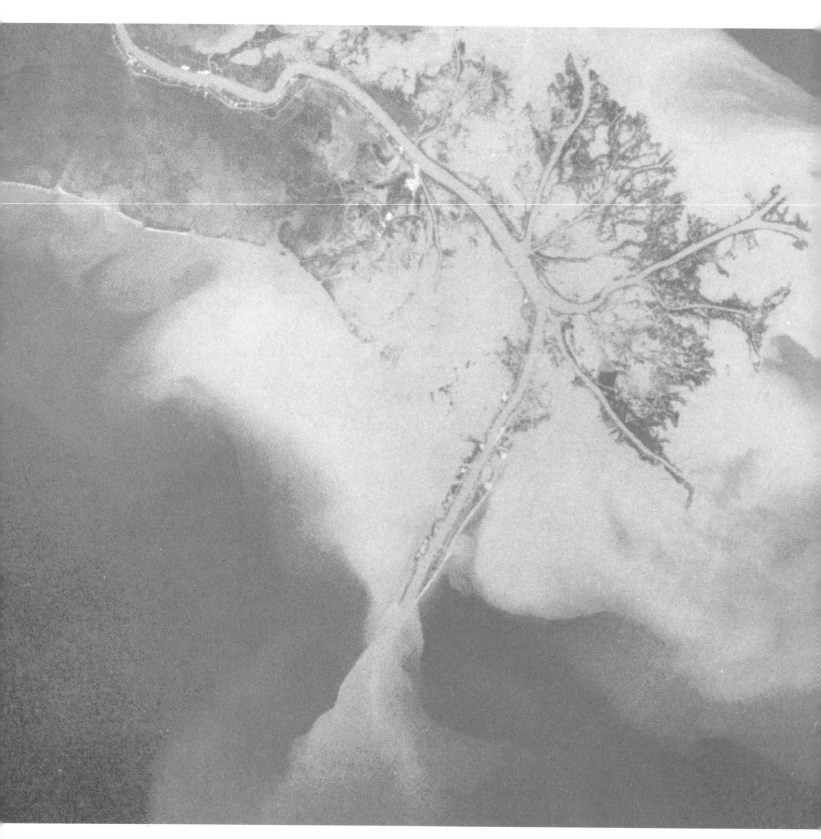

THE DELTA OF THE MISSISSIPPI, SHOWN IN A SATELLITE IMAGE (ABOVE) AND ON A MAP (RIGHT), IS A WATERY LAND, BUILT OF SEDIMENT DROPPED BY THE RIVER IN EARLIER DAYS.

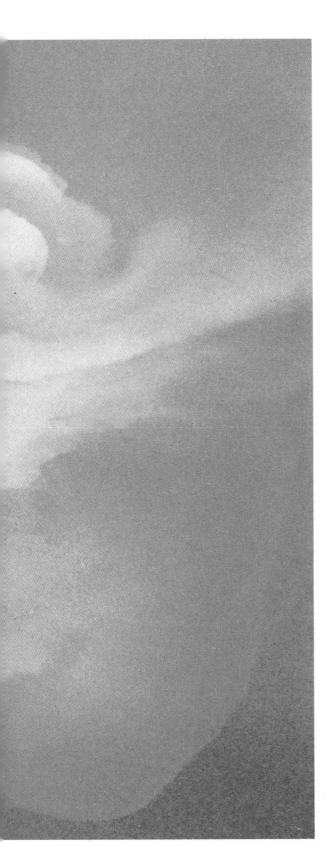

# 4
# A New Route to the Gulf?

WHEN A BIG RIVER REACHES THE SEA, it slows. Slowing, it drops the sediment it is carrying. Over time, the sediment builds up into land that is called a delta. To go on reaching the sea, the river carves a channel through the delta. Because the river goes on dropping sediment, the channel becomes choked. The river twists and turns on its way to the sea. Its course grows longer, its flow slower.

Rivers always seek the shortest route to the sea. And so the big river starts sending more of its flow down some small river upstream. This river is not a tributary. Instead of adding water

LOUISIANA

*Mississippi*

*MISSISSIPPI DELTA*

GULF OF MEXICO

N

*Oil refineries and chemical plants crowd the riverbanks from Baton Rouge south.*

to the main stream, it takes water out. In time the smaller river captures the main stream. Once the main stream changes its route to the sea, a new delta starts to form.

By changing its route, the Mississippi has formed at least six deltas in the last ten thousand years—and built coastal Louisiana. By the 1950s, the Mississippi was on the way to changing its route again, to taking a shorter, steeper route to the Gulf. That route was the Atchafalaya, which meets the Mississippi north of Baton Rouge. From there, the Atchafalaya speeds 140 miles to the Gulf. The Mississippi itself lumbers along 330 miles before spilling into the Gulf.

If the Atchafalaya captured the Mississippi, New Orleans would lose its freshwater supply. So would the oil refineries and chemical plants that line the river between New Orleans and Baton Rouge. All take huge amounts of water from the river and also need the Mississippi for shipping. Along the Atchafalaya and its floodplain, tens of thousands of people would lose homes. Bridges, highways, and power lines would be destroyed. So would pipelines that carry oil and gas from drill sites in the Gulf.

*The base of an oil rig travels by barge out into the Gulf of Mexico.*
*The drilling platform will go on top of it.*

# A Change in Course

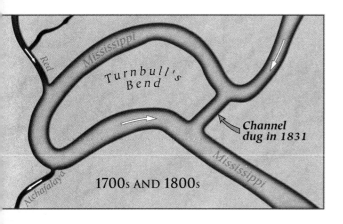

1700s AND 1800s

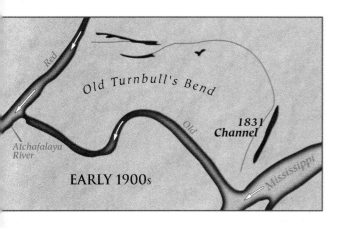

EARLY 1900s

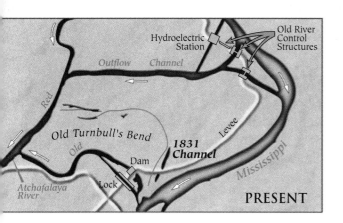

PRESENT

Congress ordered the Corps of Engineers to keep the Mississippi in its channel. The Corps set to work. It was dealing with a problem that began years earlier. In the early 1800s, the Mississippi made a huge loop 80 miles above Baton Rouge. The loop was known as Turnbull's Bend. Here the Red River flowed into the Mississippi. Here, too, the Atchafalaya set off to the Gulf. At the time, the Atchafalaya was a small stream choked by an ancient log jam 30 miles long.

In 1831 a riverboat captain became tired of steaming around the loop. He had a channel dug across Turnbull's Bend. The Mississippi accepted the channel and flowed through it toward the Gulf. But only the upper section of the loop dried up. The lower part went on flowing, and it linked the Mississippi with the two smaller rivers. The link was named Old River.

In 1839 the state of Louisiana cleared out the log jam. The Atchafalaya then flowed much better. In a way, it flowed too well, for it now offered the Mississippi a shorter, steeper route to the Gulf. The Mississippi began sending more water down the Atchafalaya.

With more water, the Atchafalaya widened and deepened—and took more water. By 1950 nearly one third of the Mississippi's water was going down the Atchafalaya. Before long, the Atchafalaya seemed likely to capture nearly all the water.

To prevent this, the Corps plugged the eastern end of Old River. It built a dam of earth that was one hundred feet high and weighed five million tons. Part of the dam was a lock,

*Steamboat races were popular events of the 1800s. Here,* Queen of the West *is in a close race with* Morning Star.

which was used by boats needing to pass through.

A few miles upstream, the Corps dug a new channel linking the Mississippi with the Red and Atchafalaya Rivers. It also built a large concrete structure with gates, named the Old River Control. The gates controlled the amount of water entering the channel from the Mississippi.

45

*A rising sun burns away early morning mist over a bayou,
where fishermen are already casting their lines.*

Congress set the amount of water that was to pass through the Old River and down the Atchafalaya. It was to be the same as it was in the 1950s: 30 percent of the combined flows of the Mississippi and Red Rivers. The amount was small enough to keep the river from changing its course. It was big enough to supply water to towns along the Atchafalaya and to the swamps and the streams, or bayous, that run through them. Finally, the Old River Control would act as a safety valve. In time of flood, water could be drawn off the Mississippi here.

The 1950s and 1960s were quiet years in the Mississippi Valley, with no big floods. Yet during this time, sediment kept building up in the main channel. Between the levees, there was less room for water than before. High water would flow higher than ever when a flood came. It came in 1973.

During autumn of 1972 and winter of 1973 the river was higher than normal. Deep winter snows fell in the upper valley. Spring brought melting snow to the north and heavy rains to the south. Water poured off the land and into the tributaries. Computer models warned that the main levees could not hold the flood that was to come. Sandbags were hastily added to 800 miles of levees. And still the rain was falling, as much as 20 inches in a day and a half.

Floodwaters rolled down the river. At Old River Control, the Mississippi piled up into a slab of water the height of a six-story building. Water raged through open gates, torn white as it tumbled into the channel below. The whole

*The Old River Control was designed to keep the Mississippi from sending most of its water down the Atchafalaya.*

structure was shaking. All gates were opened to lessen the battering. But the shaking increased.

No one could see what was happening underwater. There, swirling water was digging holes in the sediment under the Old River Control. One hole was larger and deeper than a football stadium.

On an April evening, part of the Old River Control slipped into the river, sank, and broke. The sediment beneath it had been scoured away.

The rest of the structure held. If it had failed, 70 percent of the Mississippi would have shot down the Atchafalaya. There would have been no turning back.

The Corps began studying the damage. It bored holes in the structure and lowered television cameras through them. In places the cameras found only water. Sediment had been swept away, and fish were swimming beneath the Old River Control.

Repairs were difficult. The structure stood on pilings that reached down

*After part of the Old River Control was undermined in 1973,
the Corps built a second structure to relieve pressure on the first.*

through 90 feet of sediment. It could not be anchored to bedrock; the nearest rock was 7,000 feet down—more than a mile—buried under sediment that the river had piled up. For three and a half years, the Corps filled holes with cement and other materials and dumped in huge rocks. But the repairs did not make the Old River Control as good as new. So the Corps dug another channel from the Mississippi and built a second control structure to take the pressure off the first.

At the time this book was written, the newest control structure had not been tested by a great flood. But many people wonder what might have taken place in 1993 if the tributaries of the lower Mississippi had also been in flood. As it happened, they were not. But a number of scientists and engineers think we need to find still more ways of dealing with the mighty river.

*Heavy, bulky cargoes travel the Mississippi aboard fleets of barges that are linked together and pushed by a sturdy towboat.*

# 5
# Rethinking the Mississippi

TODAY, SEVEN MILLION PEOPLE LIVE and work along the Mississippi. Most of the work is somehow linked to the river—to the rich soil, to refineries and chemical plants, to businesses that supply farms and industries or handle their products.

The Mississippi and its tributaries are a water highway for heavy, bulky cargoes carried on barges. Ports on the lower Mississippi are among the busiest in the United States. Through them pass products of the heartland—coal, grain, steel, automobiles. Through them pass supplies for farms, cities, and factories upstream—oil and gasoline, fertilizer, cement, ores, coffee.

Everything depends on managing the river. Dredges and snag boats keep the Mississippi open to shipping. Levees and flood-ways keep it off the floodplain. Levees, dams, and spillways hold the Mississippi on its course past Baton Rouge and New Orleans.

Still, efforts to keep the river in its channel do not always work as planned.

# THE UPPER VALLEY

The 1993 flood was the worst ever known north of Cairo. It erased whole towns, made islands out of peninsulas, and swallowed up roads and bridges. Small ferries had to be trucked in from Florida so that people could cross the Mississippi between home and job.

Most of the levees built by the Corps stood firm during the flood. But from southern Minnesota to Missouri, 70 percent of the other levees failed.

The Corps had built reservoirs to draw water off tributaries and store it. But except in Iowa, the torrents of rain did not fall where the reservoirs were. Even in Iowa, so much rain fell that the reservoirs filled. Some water had to be let out to keep dams from breaking and causing even worse floods.

Life on the floodplain will always be risky, but there are ways of making it less risky. For years, scientists have been saying that we have taken too much for ourselves, that we have penned up the river too much. The time has come, they say, to give the river back some of its floodplain. Flooding is a natural thing for the river to do—it needs places to go, places where it can spread out.

After the 1993 flood, the federal government started making some changes. It offered to buy whole towns or parts of towns and move them to higher ground. Buying towns would cost less than to keep rebuilding levees and paying for flood relief. By early 1995, 8,000 families had sold their houses, barns, and stores and moved to higher ground.

The government built no new levees. In areas where few people lived, it did not repair levees. Instead, it bought some farms and turned them into floodplain. It also bought

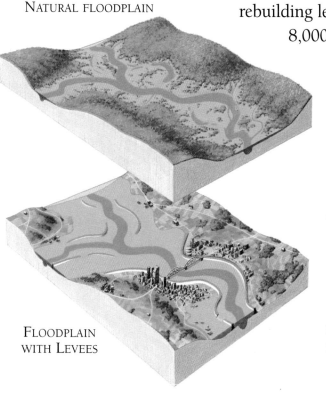

NATURAL FLOODPLAIN

FLOODPLAIN WITH LEVEES

On a natural floodplain (top), the swollen river can spread out slowly, dropping rich sediment. The land soaks up some water and holds the rest until it can drain off. Crests are likely to be lower. Squeezed between levees built to protect cities (bottom), the river swells upstream, where it may top and destroy earthen levees built to protect farmland. The river also runs faster and deeper, putting strain on levees downstream.

*Mallard ducks rocket out of their wintering ground in a wildlife refuge.*

easements from farmers; this meant farmers could work their land but would be paid to let it flood at times of high water.

Would these changes help? The answer was yes, and it came sooner than anyone had expected. In the spring of 1995, weeks of heavy rain again brought flooding to the Middle West. The same towns were threatened. Some again found themselves underwater. But this time damage and loss of life were much smaller. It is true that the amount of water that went down the river was much smaller than in 1993. Yet, it is also true that many towns-people had moved away from the danger zones and that the river could spread over more of its floodplain.

When the river can spread out, floods do less damage. In the future, plants and animals will also benefit from the change. Trees will again take root. There can be fish and wildlife refuges on the floodplain. Birds and mammals will live and feed there during dry times of year. At high water, these creatures will move to dry ground, and fish will move into the flooded areas to spawn and feed. Waterfowl, such as ducks, will fly in to nest and feed. When water drains off the land, fish will return to the river and birds and mammals to the floodplain.

# The Lower Valley

The lower Mississippi is huge, and the people who wrestle with it face some huge problems.

Left alone, the river would change its route to the Gulf. So far, the Corps of Engineers has kept it from sending its water down the Atchafalaya. But many scientists think that sooner or later the river will win. Perhaps, they say, a huge flood will overcome the controls at Old River. Or perhaps the river will swing west at some other point. But change it will.

The Corps does not agree. Given the money to do the job, it says it can hold the river in today's channel.

Either way, there are big problems.

Suppose the Mississippi shifts. Then the country will face a huge decision: Should the Mississippi be put back in its channel? The job would take

*Some people live among the bayous. Others have camps (below) that they use for work or sport.*

years of work and cost billions of dollars, but much is at stake.

Suppose the Mississippi can be kept as it now is. Then another problem will become worse. This one has to do with Louisiana's coastal marshes, land that formed as the Mississippi built its deltas. The marshes are being lost because sea levels are rising, old land is sinking, and little new land is being built.

Seas have been rising since the end of the last ice age, about ten thousand years ago. As ice caps and glaciers melt on land, their water drains into the seas. The seas rise less than an inch a year, but over years, inches add up.

Coastal Louisiana is sinking because it is made of sediment. Over time, sediment packs down—and so it shrinks and sinks. Most of New Orleans, for example, now lies at or below sea level. In places, the Mississippi is like an elevated highway that runs through the city—look up and you see the hulls of passing ships.

*Because of levees, sediment no longer builds the Mississippi Delta but shoots into the Gulf,
where it is lost to deep water or carried away by currents.*

The Mississippi used to drop enough sediment to make up for shrinking land and rising sea levels. Today, walled between levees, the Mississippi no longer builds new land. Its sediment shoots into the Gulf and is lost to deep water. New land is forming at the mouth of the Atchafalaya, but it does not equal what is being lost.

Canals make matters worse. Over the years some ten thousand miles of canals have been dredged in coastal Louisiana. They were dredged to serve hunters, fishermen, pleasure boats, oil- and gas-drilling sites in the Gulf. Once dredged, the canals widened on their own, eating away at the region from the inside. Hurricanes and tropical storms add to the damage.

Today Louisiana is losing 50 square miles of marsh a year. Unless some-

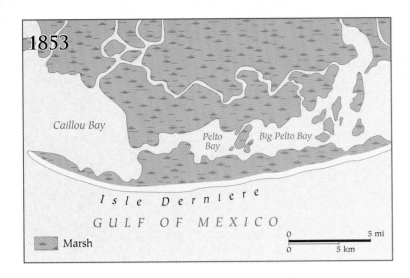

1853

Caillou Bay

Pelto Bay

Big Pelto Bay

*I s l e   D e r n i e r e*

GULF OF MEXICO

Marsh

0          5 mi

0          5 km

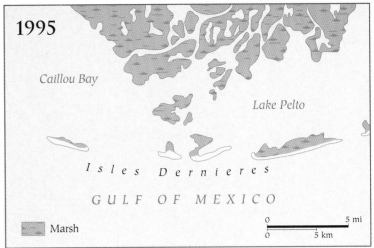

1995

Caillou Bay

Lake Pelto

*I s l e s   D e r n i e r e s*

GULF OF MEXICO

Marsh

0          5 mi

0          5 km

thing changes, it will lose an area the size of Rhode Island over the next 25 years.

The marshes are important to people who live in them among the bayous, to people who hunt and fish in them. They are also important to the rest of us. Every year fishing boats catch two billion pounds of seafood in the Gulf of Mexico. Almost every fish and shellfish caught

LOUISIANA IS LOSING ITS COASTAL MARSHES TO THE GULF OF MEXICO.

Area of moderate to severe land loss

Area Enlarged

*Fisherman unloads a catch near the delta of the Atchafalaya.*

*Alligators (above) are among the many types of animals that make their homes in the marshes of coastal Louisiana. The fields of an Iowa farm (right) hug the Mississippi River.*

in the Gulf spends part of its life in the Louisiana marshes. For many kinds, the marshes are a nursery, where the young hatch out and spend the early part of their lives.

The marshes are home to alligators and wading birds, to more shrimp and crawfish than almost any other place in the world. They are a winter home or refueling stop for millions of birds that migrate north and south along the Mississippi.

The marshes of Louisiana are much more than just some watery land.

What can be done? There are no easy answers.

No one thinks we should put things back the way they were when the Mississippi ran free.

Yet we have wrestled long and hard with the Mississippi, and the river still threatens to go its own way.

In time, answers will be found. Somehow, they must protect the people who need and use the river's floodplain, deltas, and water. Somehow they must also give the river more freedom to do what it does naturally, to flood and to build. The answers will be found in working with the Mississippi, in understanding the Mississippi as part of nature—as a mighty river and a builder of land.

*A great egret rises from its nesting ground in swampland of the Atchafalaya basin, which is home to 300 kinds of birds.*

*The buildings of a farm in La Grange, Missouri, are reflected in the floodwaters of the Mississippi.*

# ILLUSTRATION CREDITS

# INDEX

Illustrations are indicated by **boldface**. If illustrations are included within a page span, the entire span is **boldface**.

**PATRICIA LAUBER** combines her own vividly written texts and carefully chosen photographs or illustrations in such award-winning titles as the Newbery Honor Book, *Volcano: The Eruption and Healing of Mount St. Helens.* Appreciations of the author's approach to nonfiction include these comments about three of her many ALA Notable Books: "nonfiction at its best" (*Seeing Earth From Space*), "the state of the art" (*The News About Dinosaurs*), and "science at its finest—it is captivating, beautifully designed, and it both answers and evokes questions" (*Dinosaurs Walked Here and Other Stories Fossils Tell*).

Most recently, *How Dinosaurs Came to Be* received a pointer review from *Kirkus*, which called it "an exquisite prelude to the rest of the dinosaur canon."

Patricia Lauber and her husband live in Weston, Connecticut.